COOKING FOR TODAY

Baking

cinnamon & currant loaf

makes one loaf

⅔ cup butter, diced, plus extra
   for greasing

2¾ cups all-purpose flour

pinch of salt

1 tbsp baking powder

1 tbsp ground cinnamon

¾ cup brown sugar

¾ cup currants

finely grated rind of 1 orange

5–6 tbsp orange juice

6 tbsp milk

2 eggs, beaten lightly

1 Grease a 2-lb/900-g loaf pan with butter and line the base with baking parchment.

2 Strain the flour, salt, baking powder, and ground cinnamon into a bowl. Rub in the butter with your fingertips until the mixture resembles bread crumbs.

3 Stir in the sugar, currants, and orange rind. Beat the orange juice, milk, and eggs together and add to the dry ingredients. Mix well.

4 Spoon the mixture into the prepared pan. Make a dip in the center to help the loaf rise evenly.

5 Bake the loaf in a preheated oven, 350°F/180°C, for about 1–1 hour 10 minutes, or until a fine metal skewer inserted into the center of the loaf comes out clean.

6 Let the loaf cool before turning it out of the pan. Transfer to a wire rack and let cool completely before slicing.

COOK'S TIP

Once you have added the liquid to the dry ingredients, work as quickly as possible because the baking powder is activated by the liquid.

banana & cranberry loaf

makes one loaf

1 tbsp butter, for greasing

1¼ cups self-rising flour

½ tsp baking powder

¾ cup brown sugar

2 bananas, mashed

⅓ cup chopped candied peel

2 tbsp chopped mixed nuts

¼ cup dried cranberries

5–6 tbsp orange juice

2 eggs, beaten lightly

⅔ cup sunflower oil

¾ cup confectioners' sugar, strained

grated rind of 1 orange

COOK'S TIP
This tea bread will keep for a couple of days. Wrap it carefully and store in a cool, dry place.

1 Grease a 2-lb/900-g loaf pan with the butter and line the base with baking parchment.

2 Strain the flour and baking powder into a mixing bowl. Stir in the sugar, bananas, chopped candied peel, nuts, and cranberries.

3 Stir the orange juice, eggs, and oil together, until thoroughly blended. Add the mixture to the dry ingredients and mix well. Pour the mixture into the prepared pan and level the surface with a spatula.

4 Bake in a preheated oven, 350°F/180°C, for about 1 hour, until firm to the touch or until a fine metal skewer inserted into the center of the loaf comes out clean.

5 Turn out the loaf onto a wire rack and let cool completely.

6 Mix the confectioners' sugar with a little water and drizzle the frosting over the loaf. Sprinkle orange rind over the top. Let the frosting set before serving the loaf in slices.

banana & date loaf

makes one loaf

⅓ cup butter, diced, plus extra
    for greasing

generous 1½ cups self-rising flour

⅓ cup superfine sugar

⅔ cup chopped pitted dried dates

2 bananas, mashed coarsely

2 eggs, beaten lightly

2 tbsp honey

1 Grease a 2-lb/900-g loaf pan and line with baking parchment.

2 Strain the flour into a mixing bowl. Rub the butter into the flour with your fingertips until the mixture resembles fine bread crumbs.

3 Add the sugar, chopped dates, bananas, beaten eggs, and honey to the dry ingredients. Mix together to form a pourable consistency.

4 Spoon the mixture into the prepared loaf pan and level the surface with a spatula.

5 Bake the loaf in a preheated oven, 325°F/160°C for about, 1 hour, or until golden brown and a fine metal skewer inserted into the center of the loaf comes out clean.

6 Let the loaf cool for 10 minutes before turning out of the pan, then transfer to a wire rack to cool.

7 Serve the loaf warm or cold, cut into thick slices.

VARIATION

Substitute other dried fruit, such as prunes or apricots, for the dates. Use no-soak varieties for the best results.

fruit loaf with apple spread

makes one loaf

1 tbsp butter, for greasing

2 cups rolled oats

1 tsp ground cinnamon

½ cup light brown sugar

⅔ cup golden raisins

1 cup seedless raisins

2 tbsp malt extract

1¼ cups unsweetened apple juice

1¼ cups whole-wheat flour

3 tsp baking powder

FRUIT SPREAD

1½ cups strawberries, washed

　and hulled

　eating apples, cored, chopped,

　　and mixed with 1 tbsp

　　lemon juice

1¼ cups unsweetened

　　apple juice

TO SERVE

strawberries

apple wedges

1 Grease and line a 2-lb/900-g loaf pan. Place the oats, sugar, cinnamon, raisins, and malt extract in a bowl. Pour in the apple juice, stir, and let soak for 30 minutes.

2 Strain in the flour and baking powder, adding any bran that remains in the strainer, and fold in using a metal spoon.

3 Spoon the mixture into the pan and bake in a preheated oven, 350°F/180°C, for 1½ hours, until a fine metal skewer inserted into the center of the loaf comes out clean.

4 Let the loaf stand for 10 minutes, then turn out onto a wire rack and let cool completely.

5 Meanwhile, to make the fruit spread, place the strawberries and apples in a pan and pour in the apple juice. Bring the mixture to a boil,

cover, and simmer gently for 30 minutes. Beat the sauce well, then spoon into a sterilized, warmed jar. Let the sauce cool completely, then seal and label the jar.

6 Serve the fruit loaf cut into slices with 1–2 tablespoons of the fruit spread and an assortment of strawberries and apple wedges.

chocolate bread

makes one loaf

1 tbsp butter, for greasing

3½ cups strong white bread flour,
  plus extra for dusting

¼ cup unsweetened cocoa

1 tsp salt

1 envelope active dry yeast

2 tbsp brown sugar

1 tbsp oil

1¼ cups lukewarm water

1 Lightly grease a 2-lb/900-g loaf pan with the butter.

2 Strain the flour and unsweetened cocoa into a mixing bowl. Stir in the salt, dry yeast, and sugar.

3 Pour in the oil with the water and mix the ingredients together to form a dough.

4 Place the dough on a lightly floured counter and knead for 5 minutes. Alternatively, use an electric mixer with a dough hook.

5 Place the dough in a greased bowl, cover, and let rise in a warm place for about 1 hour, or until it has doubled in size.

6 Punch down the dough lightly for 1 minute, then shape it into a loaf. Place in the prepared pan, cover, and let rise in a warm place for another 30 minutes.

7 Bake in a preheated oven, 400°F/200°C, for 25–30 minutes. When the loaf is cooked, it should sound hollow when tapped on the base.

8 Transfer the bread to a wire rack and let cool completely. Cut into slices and serve.

7

date & honey loaf

makes one loaf

1 tbsp butter, for greasing

1¾ cups strong white bread flour

½ cup brown bread flour

½ tsp salt

1 envelope active dry yeast

generous ¾ cup lukewarm water

3 tbsp sunflower oil

3 tbsp honey

½ cup chopped pitted dates

2 tbsp sesame seeds

COOK'S TIP

If you cannot find a warm

place, sit a bowl with the dough

in it over a pan of warm

water and cover.

---

1 Grease a 2-lb/900-g loaf pan with the butter.

2 Strain both types of flour into a large mixing bowl, and stir in the salt and dry yeast. Pour in the lukewarm water, sunflower oil, and honey. Bring together to form a dough.

3 Place the dough on a lightly floured counter and knead for about 5 minutes, until smooth.

4 Place the dough in a greased bowl, cover, and let rise in a warm place for about 1 hour, or until doubled in size.

5 Knead in the dates and sesame seeds. Shape the dough and place in the pan.

6 Cover and stand in a warm place for a further 30 minutes, or until springy to the touch.

7 Bake in a preheated oven, 425°F/220°C, for 30 minutes. When the loaf is cooked, it should sound hollow when tapped.

8 Transfer the loaf to a wire rack and let cool completely. Serve cut into thick slices.

mango twist bread

makes one loaf

3 tbsp butter, diced, plus extra
   for greasing

3½ cups strong white bread flour,
   plus extra for dusting

1 tsp salt

1 envelope active dry yeast

1 tsp ground ginger

¼ cup brown sugar

1 small mango, peeled, pitted, and
   blended to a paste

1 cup lukewarm water

2 tbsp honey

⅔ cup golden raisins

1 egg, beaten lightly

confectioners' sugar, for dusting

1 Grease a cookie sheet with a little butter. Strain the flour and salt into a mixing bowl, stir in the dry yeast, ginger, and brown sugar and rub in the butter with your fingertips until the mixture resembles bread crumbs.

2 Stir in the mango paste, lukewarm water, and honey and bring together to form a dough.

3 Place the dough on a lightly floured counter. Knead for about 5 minutes, until smooth. Alternatively, use an electric mixer with a dough hook. Place the dough in a greased bowl, cover, and let rise in a warm place for about 1 hour, until it has doubled in size.

4 Knead in the golden raisins and shape the dough into 2 sausage shapes, each 10 inches/25 cm long. Carefully twist the 2 pieces together and pinch the ends to seal. Place the dough on the cookie sheet, cover, and leave in a warm place for another 40 minutes.

5 Brush the loaf with the egg and bake in a preheated oven, 425°F/220°C, for 30 minutes, or until golden. Let cool on a wire rack. Dust with confectioners' sugar before serving.

COOK'S TIP
You can tell when the bread is cooked because it will sound hollow when tapped.

citrus bread

makes one loaf

4 tbsp butter, diced, plus extra
   for greasing

3½ cups strong white bread flour,
   plus extra for dusting

½ tsp salt

¼ cup superfine sugar

1 envelope active dry yeast

5–6 tbsp orange juice

4 tbsp lemon juice

3–4 tbsp lime juice

⅔ cup lukewarm water

1 orange

1 lemon

1 lime

2 tbsp honey, for glazing

1 Lightly grease a cookie sheet with a little butter.

2 Strain the flour and salt into a large mixing bowl. Stir in the sugar and dry yeast.

3 Rub in the butter with your fingertips until the mixture resembles bread crumbs. Add all of the fruit juices and the water and bring together with your fingers to form a dough.

4 Place the dough on a lightly floured counter and knead for 5 minutes. Alternatively, use an electric mixer with a dough hook. Place the dough in a greased bowl, cover, and let rise in a warm place for 1 hour, until doubled in size.

5 Meanwhile, grate the rind of the orange, lemon, and lime. Knead the fruit rinds into the dough.

6 Divide the dough into 2 balls, making one slightly bigger than the other.

7 Place the larger ball on the cookie sheet and set the smaller one on top.

8 Push a floured finger through the center of the dough. Cover and let rise for about 40 minutes, or until springy to the touch.

9 Bake in a preheated oven, 425°F/220°C, for 35 minutes. Remove from the oven and transfer to a wire rack. Glaze with the honey and let cool completely.

crown loaf

makes one loaf

2 tbsp butter, diced, plus extra
   for greasing
generous 1½ cups strong white
   bread flour, plus extra for dusting
½ tsp salt
1 envelope active dry yeast
½ cup lukewarm milk
1 egg, beaten lightly
FILLING
4 tbsp butter, softened
¼ cup brown sugar
2 tbsp chopped hazelnuts
1 tbsp chopped preserved ginger
⅓ cup candied peel
1 tbsp rum or brandy
1 cup confectioners' sugar
2 tbsp lemon juice

1 Grease a cookie sheet with a little butter. Strain the flour and salt into a large mixing bowl. Stir in the yeast. Rub in the butter with your fingertips. Add the milk and egg and bring together with your fingers to form a dough.

2 Place the dough in a greased bowl, cover, and stand in a warm place for about 40 minutes, until doubled in size. Punch down the dough lightly for 1 minute, then roll out into a rectangle measuring 12 x 9 inches/30 x 23 cm.

3 To make the filling, cream the butter and sugar together in a large bowl until light and fluffy. Stir in the hazelnuts, ginger, candied peel, and rum or brandy. Spread the filling over the dough, leaving a 1-inch/2.5-cm border around the edges.

4 Roll up the dough, starting from one of the long edges, into a sausage shape. Cut into slices at 2-inch/5-cm intervals and place the slices in a circle on the cookie sheet, sides just touching. Cover and stand in a warm place to rise for 30 minutes.

5 Bake in a preheated oven, 325°F/190°C, for 20–30 minutes or until golden. Meanwhile, mix the confectioners' sugar with enough lemon juice to form a thin frosting.

6 Let the loaf cool slightly before drizzling with frosting. Let the frosting set slightly before serving.

cranberry muffins

makes eighteen

1 tbsp butter, for greasing

generous 1½ cups all-purpose flour

2 tsp baking powder

½ tsp salt

¼ cup superfine sugar

4 tbsp butter, melted

2 eggs, beaten lightly

generous ¾ cup milk

1 cup fresh cranberries

scant ½ cup freshly grated
   Parmesan cheese

1 Lightly grease 2 muffin pans with a little butter. Strain the flour, baking powder, and salt into a mixing bowl. Stir in the superfine sugar.

2 In a separate bowl, combine the butter, beaten eggs, and milk, then pour into the bowl of dry ingredients. Mix lightly together until all of the ingredients are evenly blended, then stir in the cranberries.

3 Divide the mixture among the prepared pans.

4 Sprinkle the grated Parmesan cheese over the top of each portion of the muffin mixture.

5 Bake in a preheated oven, 400°F/200°C, for 20 minutes, or until the muffins are well risen and golden brown.

6 Let the muffins cool slightly in the pans for 10 minutes, then transfer them to a wire rack, and let cool completely.

cinnamon swirls

makes twelve

2 tbsp butter, diced, plus extra
    for greasing
generous 1½ cups strong white
    bread flour, plus extra for dusting
½ tsp salt
1 envelope active dry yeast
1 egg, beaten lightly
½ cup lukewarm milk
2 tbsp maple syrup
FILLING
4 tbsp butter, softened
2 tsp ground cinnamon
¼ cup brown sugar
⅓ cup currants

1 Grease a 9-inch/23-cm square baking pan with a little butter.

2 Strain the flour and salt into a mixing bowl. Stir in the dry yeast. Rub in the butter with your fingertips until the mixture resembles bread crumbs. Add the egg and milk and bring together with your fingers to form a dough.

3 Form the dough into a ball, place in a greased bowl, cover, and let stand in a warm place for about 40 minutes, or until doubled in size.

4 Punch down the dough lightly for 1 minute, then roll out to a rectangle measuring 12 x 9 inches/ 30 x 23 cm.

5 To make the filling, cream the softened butter, cinnamon, and brown sugar together in a bowl until light and fluffy. Spread the filling evenly over the dough rectangle, leaving a 1-inch/2.5-cm border around the edges. Sprinkle the currants evenly over the top.

6 Roll up the dough from one of the long edges, and press down to seal. Cut the roll into 12 slices. Place them in the pan, cover, and let rise in a warm place for 30 minutes.

7 Bake in a preheated oven, 375°F/190°C, for 20–30 minutes, or until well risen. Brush with the syrup and let cool slightly before serving.

crunchy fruit cake

serves eight

⅓ cup butter, softened, plus extra
   for greasing
½ cup superfine sugar
2 eggs, beaten lightly
generous ⅓ cup self-rising
   flour, strained
1 tsp baking powder
⅔ cup cornmeal
1⅓ cups mixed dried fruit
¼ cup pine nuts
grated rind of 1 lemon
4 tbsp lemon juice
2 tbsp milk

VARIATION

To give a crumblier, lighter fruit
cake, omit the cornmeal and use
a generous 1 cup of self-rising
flour instead.

---

1 Grease a 7-inch/18-cm cake pan
with a little butter and line the
base with baking parchment.

2 Whisk the butter and sugar
together in a bowl until light
and fluffy.

3 Whisk in the beaten eggs, a little
at a time, whisking thoroughly
after each addition.

4 Gently fold the flour, baking
powder, and cornmeal into the
mixture until well blended.

5 Stir in the mixed dried fruit, pine
nuts, grated lemon rind, lemon
juice, and milk.

6 Spoon the mixture into the pan
and level the surface.

7 Bake in a preheated oven,
350°F/180°C, for about 1 hour, or
until a fine metal skewer inserted into
the center of the cake comes out clean.

8 Let the cake cool in the pan
before turning out.

clementine cake

serves eight

¾ cup butter, softened, plus extra
   for greasing
2 clementines
¾ cup superfine sugar
3 eggs, beaten lightly
1¼ cups self-rising flour
3 tbsp ground almonds
3 tbsp light cream
GLAZE AND TOPPING
6 tbsp clementine juice
2 tbsp superfine sugar
3 white sugar lumps, crushed

COOK'S TIP

If you like, chop the rind
from the clementines in a
food processor or blender
with the sugar in step 2. Tip
the mixture into a bowl
with the butter and begin
to cream the mixture.

1 Grease a 7-inch/18-cm round pan
with a little butter and line the
base with baking parchment.

2 Pare the rind from the clementines
and chop it finely. Cream the
butter, sugar, and clementine rind
together in a bowl until pale and fluffy.

3 Gradually add the beaten eggs to
the mixture, beating thoroughly
after each addition.

4 Gently fold in the flour, ground
almonds, and light cream. Spoon
the mixture into the prepared pan.

5 Bake in a preheated oven,
350°F/180°C, for 55–60 minutes,
or until a fine metal skewer inserted
into the center comes out clean. Let
cool for 10 minutes.

6 Meanwhile, to make the glaze,
put the clementine juice into a
small pan with the superfine sugar.
Bring to a boil over low heat and
simmer for 5 minutes.

7 Turn out the cake onto a wire
rack. Drizzle the glaze over the
cake until it has been absorbed and
sprinkle with the crushed sugar lumps.
Let cool completely before serving.

caraway madeira

serves eight

1 cup butter, softened, plus extra
for greasing
scant 1 cup brown sugar
3 eggs, beaten lightly
2½ cups self-rising flour
1 tbsp caraway seeds
grated rind of 1 lemon
6 tbsp milk
1 or 2 strips of citron peel

1 Grease a 2-lb/900-g loaf pan and line with baking parchment.

2 Cream the butter and brown sugar together in a bowl until pale and fluffy.

3 Gradually add the beaten eggs to the creamed mixture, beating well after each addition.

4 Strain the flour into the bowl and gently fold into the creamed mixture with a figure-eight movement.

5 Add the caraway seeds, lemon rind, and milk, and gently fold in until thoroughly blended.

6 Spoon the mixture into the prepared pan and level the surface with a spatula.

7 Bake in a preheated oven, 325°F/160°C, for 20 minutes.

COOK'S TIP

Citron peel is available in the baking section of large stores. If it is unavailable, you can substitute chopped mixed peel.

8 Remove the cake from the oven and gently place the pieces of citron peel on top. Return to the oven and bake for 40 minutes more, or until the cake is well risen, golden, and a fine skewer inserted into the center comes out clean.

9 Let the cake cool in the pan for 10 minutes before turning out, then transfer it to a wire rack to let it cool completely.

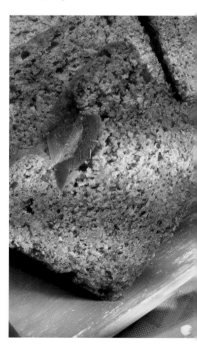

19

lemon syrup cake

serves eight

1 tbsp butter, for greasing

scant 1½ cups all-purpose flour

2 tsp baking powder

1 cup superfine sugar

4 eggs

⅔ cup sour cream

grated rind of 1 large lemon

4 tbsp lemon juice

⅔ cup sunflower oil

SYRUP

4 tbsp confectioners' sugar

3 tbsp lemon juice

1 Lightly grease an 8-inch/20-cm loose-based round cake pan with a little butter and line the base with baking parchment.

2 Strain the flour and baking powder into a large mixing bowl and stir in the sugar.

3 In a bowl or pitcher, whisk the eggs, sour cream, lemon rind, lemon juice, and oil together.

4 Pour the egg mixture into the dry ingredients and mix well until evenly blended.

5 Pour the mixture into the prepared pan and bake in a preheated oven, 350°F/180°C, for 45–60 minutes, until risen and golden on top.

6 To make the syrup, mix the confectioners' sugar and lemon juice together in a small pan. Stir over low heat until just starting to bubble and turn syrupy.

7 As soon as the cake comes out of the oven prick the surface with a fine metal skewer, then brush the syrup over the top. Let cool completely in the pan before turning out and serving.

COOK'S TIP

Pricking the surface of the hot cake with a skewer insures that the syrup seeps into the cake and the flavor is absorbed.

apple cake with cider

serves eight

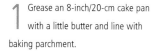

6 tbsp butter, diced, plus extra
   for greasing

generous 1½ cups self-rising flour

1 tsp baking powder

⅓ cup superfine sugar

3½ cups chopped dried apple

generous ½ cup raisins

⅔ cup sweet cider

1 egg, beaten lightly

1 cup raspberries

1 Grease an 8-inch/20-cm cake pan with a little butter and line with baking parchment.

2 Strain the flour and baking powder into a large mixing bowl and rub in the butter with your fingertips until the mixture resembles fine bread crumbs.

3 Stir in the superfine sugar, dried apple, and raisins.

4 Pour in the sweet cider and egg and mix together until thoroughly blended. Stir in the raspberries very gently so that they do not break up.

5 Pour the mixture into the prepared cake pan.

6 Bake in a preheated oven, 375°F/190°C, for 40 minutes, or until risen and lightly golden.

7 Let the cake cool in the pan for 10 minutes, then turn out onto a wire rack, and let cool completely before serving.

orange kugelhopf cake

serves four

1 cup butter, softened, plus extra
   for greasing
generous 1 cup superfine sugar
4 eggs, separated
scant 3½ cups all-purpose flour
pinch of salt
3 tsp baking powder
1¼ cups fresh orange juice
1 tbsp orange flower water
1 tsp grated orange rind
SYRUP
¾ cup orange juice
1 cup granulated sugar

1 Grease and flour a 10-inch/25-cm
   kugelhopf pan or deep ring mold.

2 Cream the butter and superfine
   sugar together in a bowl until
light and fluffy, then add the egg
yolks, 1 at a time, whisking well after
each addition.

3 Strain the flour, salt, and baking
   powder into a separate bowl.
Fold the dry ingredients and the
orange juice alternately into the
creamed mixture with a metal spoon,
working as lightly as possible. Gently
stir in the orange flower water and
orange rind.

4 Whisk the egg whites until they
   form soft peaks, then gently fold
them into the mixture using a figure-
eight movement.

5 Pour into the prepared pan or
   mold. Bake in a preheated oven,
350°F/180°C, for 50–55 minutes, or
until a fine metal skewer inserted into
the center of the cake comes out clean.

6 To make the syrup, bring the
   orange juice and sugar to a boil
in a small pan over low heat, then
simmer gently for 5 minutes, until the
sugar has dissolved.

7 Remove the cake from the
   oven and let cool in the pan for
10 minutes. Prick the top of the cake
with a fine metal skewer and brush
over half of the syrup. Let the cake
cool, still in the pan, for another
10 minutes, then invert the cake
onto a wire rack placed over a deep
plate and brush the syrup over the
cake until it is completely covered.
Serve warm or cold.

carrot & ginger cake

serves ten

1 tbsp butter, for greasing

generous 1½ cups all-purpose flour

1 tsp baking powder

1 tsp baking soda

2 tsp ground ginger

½ tsp salt

scant 1 cup light brown sugar

generous 1 cup grated carrots

2 pieces of preserved
   ginger, chopped

1 tbsp grated fresh gingerroot

⅓ cup seedless raisins

2 eggs, beaten lightly

3 tbsp corn oil

juice of 1 orange

FROSTING

1 cup lowfat soft cheese

4 tbsp confectioners' sugar

1 tsp vanilla extract

TO DECORATE

grated carrot

finely chopped preserved ginger

ground ginger

1 Grease an 8-inch/20-cm round cake pan with butter and line with baking parchment.

2 Strain the flour, baking powder, baking soda, ground ginger, and salt into a bowl. Stir in the sugar, carrots, preserved ginger, fresh ginger, and raisins. In a separate bowl, beat together the eggs, oil, and orange juice, then stir into the dry ingredients.

3 Spoon the mixture into the prepared pan and bake in a preheated oven, 350°F/180°C, for 1–1¼ hours, until firm to the touch, or until a fine metal skewer inserted into the center of the cake comes out clean. Let cool in the pan.

4 To make the frosting, place the soft cheese in a bowl and beat to soften. Sift in the confectioners' sugar and add the vanilla extract. Mix well.

5 Turn the cake out and smooth the frosting over the top. Decorate with grated carrot and preserved and ground ginger and serve.

strawberry roulade

serves eight

3 extra large eggs

⅔ cup superfine sugar

scant 1 cup all-purpose flour

1 tbsp hot water

FILLING

¾ cup mascarpone

1 tsp almond extract

1½ cups small strawberries

TO DECORATE

1 tbsp toasted sliced almonds

1 tsp confectioners' sugar

1 Line a 14 x 10-inch/35 x 25-cm jelly roll pan with baking parchment. Place the eggs in a heatproof bowl with the superfine sugar. Whisk together, then place the bowl over a pan of hot water and whisk the mixture until pale and thick.

2 Remove the bowl from the pan. Strain in the flour and fold into the egg mixture with the hot water. Pour the mixture into the prepared pan and bake in a preheated oven, 425°F/220°C, for 8–10 minutes, until golden and set.

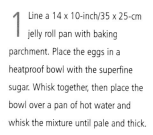

3 Remove from the oven and turn out the roulade onto a sheet of baking parchment. Peel off the lining paper and roll up the sponge cake tightly along with the baking parchment. Wrap in a dish towel and let cool.

4 To make the filling, mix together the mascarpone and almond extract. Reserve a few strawberries for decoration, then wash, hull, and slice the rest. Chill the mascarpone mixture and the strawberries in the refrigerator until required.

5 Unroll the cake, spread the mascarpone mixture over the surface, and sprinkle with sliced strawberries. Roll the cake up again and transfer to a serving plate. Sprinkle with almonds and lightly dust with confectioners' sugar. Decorate with the reserved strawberries.

25

rich fruit cake

serves four

1 tbsp butter, for greasing

generous ½ cup no-soak prunes

1 cup chopped pitted dates

generous ¾ cup unsweetened
    orange juice

2 tbsp molasses

1 tsp finely grated lemon rind

1 tsp finely grated orange rind

generous 1½ cups whole-
    wheat flour

2 tsp baking powder

1 tsp allspice

⅔ cup seedless raisins

⅔ cup golden raisins

⅔ cup currants

generous 1 cup dried cranberries

3 extra large eggs, separated

TO DECORATE

1 tbsp apricot preserve, warmed

confectioners' sugar, for dusting

generous 1 cup sugarpaste

strips of orange rind

strips of lemon rind

1 Grease a deep round 8-inch/
20-cm cake pan and line with
baking parchment. Chop the prunes,
place in a pan with the dates, pour
over the orange juice, and simmer over
low heat for 10 minutes. Remove from
the heat and beat to a paste. Stir in the
molasses and rinds. Let cool.

2 Strain the flour, baking powder
and allspice into a bowl, adding
any bran from the strainer. Add the
dried fruits. When the prune mixture
is cool, whisk in the egg yolks. In a
separate bowl, whisk the egg whites
until stiff. Spoon the fruit mixture into
the dry ingredients and mix together.

3 Gently fold in the egg whites
using a metal spoon. Transfer
to the prepared cake pan and bake
in a preheated oven, 325°F/170°C,
for 1½ hours. Let cool in the pan.

4 Turn the cake out and brush the
top with apricot preserve. Dust
the counter with confectioners' sugar
and roll out the sugarpaste thinly.
Lay the sugarpaste over the top of the
cake and trim the edges. Decorate
with citrus rind.

coconut cake

serves six—eight

½ cup butter, diced, plus extra
    for greasing

generous 1½ cups self-rising flour

pinch of salt

½ cup raw brown sugar

1 cup dry unsweetened coconut,
    plus extra for sprinkling

2 eggs, beaten lightly

4 tbsp milk

2 Strain the flour and salt into a mixing bowl and rub in the butter with your fingertips until the mixture resembles fine bread crumbs.

1 Lightly grease a 2-lb/900-g loaf pan with butter and line with baking parchment.

3 Stir in the sugar, coconut, eggs, and milk and mix to a soft consistency.

4 Spoon the mixture into the prepared loaf pan and level the surface with a spatula. Bake in a preheated oven, 325°F/160°C, for 30 minutes.

5 Remove the cake from the oven and sprinkle with the extra coconut. Return to the oven and bake for 30 minutes more, until risen and golden and a metal skewer inserted into the center comes out clean.

6 Let the cake cool slightly in the pan, then turn out, and transfer to a wire rack, and let cool completely before serving.

orange & almond cake

serves eight

1 tbsp butter, for greasing
4 eggs, separated
scant ¾ cup superfine sugar
finely grated rind and juice
   of 2 oranges
finely grated rind and juice
   of 1 lemon
generous 1 cup ground almonds
2½ tbsp self-rising flour
ORANGE-CINNAMON CREAM
generous ¾ cup whipping cream
1 tsp ground cinnamon
2 tsp caster sugar
TO DECORATE
1 tbsp toasted sliced almonds
confectioners' sugar, for dusting

VARIATION

You could serve this cake with a syrup. Boil the juice and grated rind of 2 oranges with scant ⅓ cup superfine sugar and 2 tablespoons of water for 5–6 minutes until slightly thickened. Stir in 1 tablespoon orange liqueur before serving.

1 Grease a deep 7-inch/18-cm round cake pan with butter. Line the base with baking parchment.

2 Cream the egg yolks and sugar in a bowl until the mixture is pale and thick. Whisk half of the orange rind and all of the lemon rind into the egg yolk mixture.

COOK'S TIP

When whipping cream, chill the bowl, whisk, and cream before starting. Whisk briskly until it starts to thicken and then more slowly until soft peaks form.

3 Mix the juice from the oranges and lemon with the ground almonds and stir into the egg yolk mixture. Gently fold in the flour.

4 Whisk the egg whites until stiff, then gently fold them into the egg yolk mixture.

5 Pour the mixture into the prepared pan and bake in a preheated oven, 350°F/180°C, for 35–40 minutes, or until golden and springy to the touch. Let cool in the pan for 10 minutes, then turn out and leave to cool completely.

6 Whip the cream until soft peaks form. Stir in the remaining orange rind, cinnamon and sugar. Cover the cooled cake with the sliced almonds, dust with confectioners' sugar, and serve immediately with the orange and cinnamon cream.

almond slices

makes eight

3 eggs

⅔ cup ground almonds

1½ cups dry milk

1 cup granulated sugar

½ tsp saffron threads

scant ½ cup sweet butter

1 tbsp sliced almonds, to decorate

1 Beat the eggs together in a bowl and set aside.

2 Place the ground almonds, dry milk, sugar, and saffron in a large mixing bowl and mix well.

3 Melt the butter in a small pan over low heat. Pour the melted butter over the dry ingredients and mix well until thoroughly blended.

4 Add the reserved beaten eggs to the mixture and mix well.

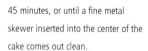

5 Spread the cake mixture evenly in a shallow 7–9-inch/15–20-cm ovenproof dish and bake in a preheated oven, 325°F/160°C, for

COOK'S TIP

These almond slices are best eaten hot, but they may also be served cold. They can be made a day or even a week in advance and reheated. They also freeze beautifully.

45 minutes, or until a fine metal skewer inserted into the center of the cake comes out clean.

6 Cut the almond cake into 8 slices. Decorate the almond slices with sliced almonds, and transfer to serving plates. Serve hot or cold.

pear & ginger cake

serves six

scant 1 cup sweet butter, softened, plus extra for greasing

generous ¾ cup superfine sugar

1¼ cups self-rising flour, strained

1 tbsp ground ginger

3 eggs, beaten lightly

1 lb/450 g pears, peeled, cored, and thinly sliced, then brushed with lemon juice

1 tbsp brown sugar

ice cream or heavy cream, lightly whipped, to serve (optional)

COOK'S TIP

Store brown sugar in an airtight container, rather than in its package, where it can absorb water from the air. If the sugar becomes hard, do not throw it away. Wrap the package in a clean, damp dish towel and heat in the microwave on Medium for 1–2 minutes, until it begins to soften.

1 Lightly grease a deep 8-inch/ 20-cm cake pan with butter and line the base with baking parchment.

2 Mix all but 2 tablespoons of the butter with the superfine sugar, flour, ginger, and eggs in a bowl. Beat with a whisk until the mixture forms a smooth consistency.

3 Spoon the cake batter into the prepared pan and level out the surface with a spatula.

4 Arrange the pear slices over the cake batter. Sprinkle with the brown sugar and dot with the remaining butter.

5 Bake in a preheated oven, 350°F/180°C, for 35–40 minutes, or until the cake is golden on top and feels springy to the touch.

6 Serve the pear and ginger cake warm, with ice cream or whipped cream, if you like.

VARIATION

For a different flavor, substitute 2 teaspoons ground cinnamon for the ground ginger and use vanilla sugar instead of plain.

coffee streusel cake

serves eight

½ cup butter, melted and cooled,
  plus extra for greasing

2 cups all-purpose flour

1 tbsp baking powder

⅓ cup superfine sugar

⅔ cup milk

2 eggs

2 tbsp instant coffee mixed with
  1 tbsp boiling water

⅓ cup chopped almonds

confectioners' sugar, for dusting

TOPPING

½ cup self-rising flour

⅓ cup raw brown sugar

2 tbsp butter, diced

1 tsp ground allspice

1 tbsp water

1 Grease a 9-inch/23-cm loose-based round cake pan with butter and line with baking parchment. Strain the flour and baking powder into a mixing bowl, then stir in the superfine sugar.

2 Whisk the milk, eggs, melted butter, and coffee mixture together and pour onto the dry ingredients. Add the chopped almonds and mix lightly together. Spoon the mixture into the prepared pan.

3 To make the topping, combine the flour and raw brown sugar in a bowl.

4 Rub in the butter with your fingertips until the mixture resembles bread crumbs. Sprinkle in the allspice and water and bring the mixture together into loose crumbs. Sprinkle evenly over the cake batter.

5 Bake the cake in a preheated oven, 375°F/190°C, for about 50 minutes–1 hour. Cover loosely with foil if the topping starts to brown too quickly. Let the cake cool in the pan, then turn out, dust with confectioners' sugar, and serve.

gingerbread

makes twelve

⅔ cup butter, plus extra
    for greasing

scant 1 cup brown sugar

2 tbsp molasses

generous 1½ cups all-
    purpose flour

1 tsp baking powder

2 tsp baking soda

2 tsp ground ginger

⅔ cup milk

1 egg, beaten lightly

2 eating apples, peeled, chopped,
    and coated with lemon juice

VARIATION

If you enjoy the flavor of
ginger, try adding 1 tablespoon
finely chopped preserved ginger
to the mixture in step 3.

---

1 Grease a 9-inch/23-cm square
cake pan with a little butter and
line with baking parchment.

2 Melt the butter, sugar, and
molasses in a pan over low heat.
Remove from the heat and let cool.

3 Strain the flour, baking powder,
baking soda, and ground ginger
together into a mixing bowl.

4 Stir in the milk, egg, and cooled
butter and molasses mixture,
followed by the chopped apples.

5 Stir gently, then pour the mixture
into the prepared pan, and level
the surface with a spatula.

6 Bake in a preheated oven,
325°F/160°C, for 30–35 minutes,
until the cake has risen and a fine
metal skewer inserted into the center
comes out clean.

7 Let the ginger cake cool in
the pan, then turn out, and cut
into 12 bars.

sugar-topped blackberry & apple cake

serves ten

1 tbsp butter, for greasing

12 oz/350 g cooking apples

3 tbsp lemon juice

generous 2 cups whole-
wheat flour

2½ tsp baking powder

1 tsp ground cinnamon, plus extra
for dusting

1 cup prepared blackberries,
thawed if frozen, plus extra
to decorate

scant 1 cup light brown sugar

1 egg, beaten lightly

¾ cup lowfat plain yogurt

2 oz/55 g white or brown sugar
lumps, crushed lightly

sliced eating apple, to decorate

VARIATION

Try replacing the blackberries
with blueberries. Use the canned
or frozen variety if fresh
blueberries are unavailable.

---

1 Grease a 2-lb/900-g loaf pan with a little butter and line with baking parchment. Core, peel, and finely dice the cooking apples. Place them in a pan with the lemon juice, bring to a boil, cover, and simmer for 10 minutes, until soft. Beat well. Set aside to cool.

2 Strain the flour, baking powder, and cinnamon into a bowl, adding any bran that remains in the strainer. Stir in ⅔ cup of the blackberries and the sugar.

3 Make a well in the center of the ingredients and add the egg, yogurt, and cooled apple paste. Mix until thoroughly blended. Spoon the mixture into the prepared loaf pan and level over the top with a spatula.

4 Sprinkle with the remaining blackberries, pressing them down into the cake batter, and top the batter with the crushed sugar lumps. Bake in a preheated oven, 375°F/190°C, for 40–45 minutes, then let cool in the pan.

5 Turn the cake out and peel away the baking parchment. Serve dusted with cinnamon and decorated with blackberries and apple slices.

dark biscuits

makes eight

6 tbsp butter, diced, plus extra
   for greasing

generous 1½ cups self-rising flour,
   plus extra for dusting

pinch of salt

1 tbsp superfine sugar

1 eating apple, peeled, cored,
   and chopped

1 egg, beaten lightly

2 tbsp molasses

5 tbsp milk

1 Lightly grease a cookie sheet
   with a little butter.

2 Strain the flour, sugar, and salt
   into a mixing bowl.

3 Add the butter and rub it in with
   your fingertips until the mixture
resembles fine bread crumbs.

4 Stir the apple into the mixture
   until thoroughly combined.

5 Combine the beaten egg,
   molasses, and milk in a pitcher.
Add to the dry ingredients and bring
together to form a soft dough.

6 Roll out the dough on a lightly
   floured counter to a thickness of
¾ inch/2 cm and stamp out 8 circles,
using a 2-inch/5-cm cutter.

7 Arrange the biscuits on the
   prepared cookie sheet and bake
in a preheated oven, 425°F/220°C, for
about 8–10 minutes.

8 Transfer the biscuits to a wire
   rack and let cool slightly. Serve
split in half and spread with butter.

apple shortcakes

serves four

2 tbsp butter, diced, plus extra
for greasing

1¼ cups all-purpose flour, plus extra
for dusting

½ tsp salt

1 tsp baking powder

1 tbsp superfine sugar

¼ cup milk

confectioners' sugar, for
dusting (optional)

FILLING

3 eating apples, peeled, cored,
and sliced

½ cup superfine sugar

1 tbsp lemon juice

1 tsp ground cinnamon

1¼ cups water

⅔ cup heavy cream, whipped lightly

1 Lightly grease a cookie sheet with a little butter. Strain the flour, salt, and baking powder into a mixing bowl. Stir in the sugar, then rub in the butter with your fingertips until the mixture resembles fine bread crumbs.

2 Pour in the milk and bring together to form a soft dough. Knead the dough lightly on a lightly

floured counter, then roll out to ½ inch/ 1 cm thick. Stamp out 4 circles, using a 2-inch/5-cm cutter. Transfer the circles to the prepared cookie sheet.

3 Bake in a preheated oven, 425°F/220°C, for 15 minutes, until risen and browned. Let cool.

4 To make the filling, place the apple slices, sugar, lemon juice, and cinnamon in a pan. Add the water, bring to a boil, and simmer, uncovered, for 5–10 minutes, until the apples are tender. Let cool a little, then remove the apples.

5 Split the shortcakes in half. Place each lower half on a serving plate and spoon a fourth of the apple slices onto each, and top with cream. Place the other half of the shortcake on top. Serve dusted with confectioners' sugar if you like.

cherry biscuits

makes eight

6 tbsp butter, diced, plus extra
   for greasing
generous 1½ cups self-rising flour,
   plus extra for dusting
1 tbsp superfine sugar
pinch of salt
3 tbsp candied cherries, chopped
3 tbsp golden raisins
1 egg, beaten lightly
scant ¼ cup milk

COOK'S TIP

These biscuits will freeze
very successfully, but they
are best thawed and eaten
within 1 month.

1 Lightly grease a cookie sheet with a little butter.

2 Strain the flour, sugar, and salt into a mixing bowl and rub in the butter with your fingertips until the mixture resembles bread crumbs.

3 Stir in the candied cherries and golden raisins. Add the egg.

4 Reserve 1 tablespoon of the milk for glazing, then add the remainder to the mixture. Bring together to form a soft dough.

5 Roll out the dough on a lightly floured counter to a thickness of ¾ inch/2 cm and cut out 8 circles, using a 2-inch/5-cm cutter.

6 Place the biscuits on the prepared cookie sheet and brush the tops with the reserved milk.

7 Bake in a preheated oven, 425°F/220°C, for 8–10 minutes, or until the biscuits are golden brown.

8 Transfer the biscuits to a wire rack and let cool. Serve split in half and spread with butter.

shortbread fantails

makes eight

½ cup butter, softened, plus extra
    for greasing
scant ¼ cup granulated sugar
2 tbsp confectioners' sugar
generous 1½ cups all-purpose flour,
    plus extra for dusting
pinch of salt
2 tsp orange flower water
superfine sugar, for sprinkling

1 Grease a shallow 8-inch/20-cm
    round cake pan with butter.

2 Cream the butter, granulated
    sugar, and confectioners' sugar
together in a large mixing bowl until
light and fluffy.

3 Strain the flour and salt into the
    creamed mixture. Add the orange
flower water and bring together with
your fingers to form a soft dough.

4 Roll out the dough on a lightly
    floured counter into an 8-inch/
20-cm circle and place in the prepared
pan. Prick well and score into
8 triangles with a round-bladed knife.

5 Bake the shortbread in a
    preheated oven, 325°F/160°C, for
30–35 minutes, or until it is crisp and
the top is pale golden.

6 Sprinkle with superfine sugar,
    then cut along the marked lines
to make the fantails.

7 Let the shortbread cool in the pan
    before serving.

3

4

4

lemon jumbles

makes fifty

⅓ cup butter, softened, plus extra
for greasing
generous ½ cup superfine sugar
grated rind of 1 lemon
1 egg, beaten lightly
4 tbsp lemon juice
2½ cups all-purpose flour, plus extra
for dusting
1 tsp baking powder
1 tbsp milk
confectioners' sugar, for dredging

VARIATION

If you prefer, form the dough into
other shapes—letters of the
alphabet or geometric designs.

---

1 Lightly grease several cookie sheets with a little butter.

2 Cream the butter, superfine sugar, and lemon rind together in a mixing bowl until pale and fluffy.

3 Add the beaten egg and lemon juice, a little at a time, beating thoroughly after each addition.

4 Strain the flour and baking powder into the mixture and mix until blended. Add the milk and bring together with your fingers to form a soft dough.

5 Turn the dough out onto a lightly floured counter and divide into about 50 equal-size pieces.

6 Roll each piece into a sausage shape with your hands and bend into an "S" shape.

7 Place the dough shapes on the prepared cookie sheets and bake in a preheated oven, 325°F/160°C, for 15–20 minutes. Transfer to a wire rack and let cool completely. Dredge generously with confectioners' sugar before serving.

gingersnaps

makes thirty

½ cup butter, plus extra for greasing

2½ cups self-rising flour

pinch of salt

1 cup superfine sugar

1 tbsp ground ginger

1 tsp baking soda

¼ cup light corn syrup

1 egg, beaten lightly

1 tsp grated orange rind

COOK'S TIP

Store these cookies in an
airtight container and eat
them within 1 week.

VARIATION

For less traditional, but equally
delicious cookies, substitute
1 tablespoon apple pie spice for
the ground ginger and
1 teaspoon finely grated lemon
rind for the orange rind.

1 Lightly grease several cookie
sheets with a little butter.

2 Strain the flour, salt, sugar,
ground ginger, and baking soda
into a large mixing bowl.

3 Put the butter and light corn
syrup into a pan and place the
pan over very low heat until the butter
has melted.

4 Remove the pan from the heat
and let the butter mixture cool
slightly, then pour the mixture onto the
dry ingredients.

5 Add the egg and orange rind and
bring together to form a dough.

6 Using your hands, carefully shape
the dough into 30 even-size balls.

7 Place the balls well apart on the
prepared cookie sheets, then
flatten them slightly with your fingers.

8 Bake in a preheated oven,
325°F/160°C, for 15–20 minutes.
Transfer the cookies to a wire rack to
cool and crispen before serving.

cinnamon & seed squares

makes twelve

generous 1 cup butter, softened,
plus extra for greasing
1¼ cups superfine sugar
3 eggs, beaten lightly
1¾ cups self-rising flour
½ tsp baking soda
1 tbsp ground cinnamon
⅔ cup sour cream
3½ oz/100 g sunflower seeds

COOK'S TIP

These moist squares will
freeze well and will keep for
up to 1 month.

1 Grease a 9-inch/23-cm square
cake pan with a little butter and
line the base with baking parchment.

2 Cream together the butter and
superfine sugar in a large
mixing bowl until the mixture is light
and fluffy.

3 Gradually add the beaten eggs to
the mixture, beating thoroughly
after each addition.

4 Strain the self-rising flour, baking
soda, and ground cinnamon
into the creamed mixture, then fold
in gently, using a metal spoon in a
figure-eight movement.

5 Spoon in the sour cream and
sunflower seeds and mix gently
until well blended.

6 Spoon the cake batter into the
prepared cake pan, then level
the surface with the back of a spoon
or a spatula.

7 Bake in a preheated oven,
350°F/180°C, for 45 minutes,
until the surface is firm to the touch
when pressed with a finger.

8 Loosen the edges with a round-
bladed knife, then turn out onto a
wire rack to cool completely. Slice into
12 squares before serving.

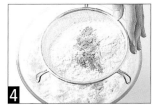

hazelnut squares

makes sixteen

⅓ cup butter, diced, plus extra
    for greasing
generous 1 cup all-purpose flour
pinch of salt
1 tsp baking powder
¾ cup brown sugar
1 egg, beaten lightly
4 tbsp milk
1 cup hazelnuts, cut into halves
raw brown sugar, for
    sprinkling (optional)

1 Grease a 9-inch/23-cm square cake pan with a little butter and line the base with baking parchment.

2 Strain the flour, salt, and the baking powder into a large mixing bowl.

3 Rub in the butter with your fingertips until the mixture resembles fine bread crumbs. Add the brown sugar to the mixture and stir to blend.

4 Add the beaten egg, milk, and nuts to the mixture and stir well until thoroughly blended and the mixture has a soft consistency.

5 Spoon the mixture into the prepared cake pan and level the surface with a spatula. Sprinkle with raw brown sugar, if you like.

6 Bake in a preheated oven, 350°F/180°C, for 25 minutes, or until the surface is firm to the touch when pressed with a finger.

7 Let cool in the pan for about 10 minutes, then loosen the edges with a round-bladed knife, and turn out onto a wire rack. Cut into 16 squares to serve.

VARIATION

For a coffee time cookie, replace the milk with the same amount of cold strong black coffee—the stronger the better.

---

oat & raisin cookies

makes ten

4 tbsp butter, plus extra for greasing

generous ½ cup superfine sugar

1 egg, lightly beaten

generous ⅓ cup all-purpose flour

½ tsp salt

½ tsp baking powder

2 cups rolled oats

¾ cup raisins

2 tbsp sesame seeds

COOK'S TIP

To enjoy these cookies at their best, store them in an airtight container.

---

1 Lightly grease 2 cookie sheets with a little butter.

2 Cream the butter and sugar together in a large mixing bowl until light and fluffy.

3 Gradually add the beaten egg, beating well after each addition until thoroughly blended.

4 Strain the flour, salt, and baking powder into the creamed mixture. Mix together gently. Add the oats, raisins, and sesame seeds, and mix together thoroughly.

5 Place 10 spoonfuls of the mixture on the prepared cookie sheets, spaced well apart to allow room to expand during cooking, and flatten them slightly with the back of a spoon.

6 Bake in a preheated oven, 350°F/180°C, for 15 minutes.

7 Let the cookies cool slightly on the cookie sheets.

8 Carefully transfer the cookies to a wire rack and let cool completely before serving.

rock drops

makes eight

⅓ cup butter, diced, plus extra
    for greasing

scant 1½ cups all-purpose flour

2 tsp baking powder

⅓ cup raw brown sugar

½ cup golden raisins

2 tbsp candied cherries,
    chopped finely

1 egg, beaten lightly

2 tbsp milk

COOK'S TIP

For convenience, prepare the dry
ingredients in advance and just
before cooking, stir in the liquid.

1 Lightly grease a cookie sheet
with a little butter.

2 Strain the flour and baking
powder into a mixing bowl. Rub
in the butter with your fingertips until
the mixture resembles bread crumbs.

3 Stir in the raw brown sugar,
raisins, and candied cherries.

4 Add the beaten egg and milk to
the mixture and bring together to
form a soft dough.

5 Spoon 8 mounds of the mixture
onto the prepared cookie sheet,
spacing them well apart to allow room
to expand during cooking.

6 Bake in a preheated oven,
400°F/200°C, for 15–20 minutes,
until firm to the touch when pressed
with a finger.

7 Remove the rock drops from the
cookie sheet. Serve piping hot
from the oven, or transfer to a wire
rack and let cool before serving.

citrus crescents

makes twenty-five

⅓ cup butter, softened, plus extra
   for greasing
⅓ cup superfine sugar, plus extra
   for dusting (optional)
1 egg, separated
scant 1½ cups all-purpose flour, plus
   extra for dusting
grated rind of 1 orange
grated rind of 1 lemon
grated rind of 1 lime
2–3 tbsp orange juice

1 Lightly grease 2 cookie sheets
with a little butter.

2 Cream the butter and sugar
together in a mixing bowl until
light and fluffy, then gradually beat in
the egg yolk.

3 Strain the flour into the creamed
mixture and mix until evenly
blended. Add the orange, lemon, and
lime rinds to the mixture, with enough
orange juice to form a soft dough.

4 Roll out the dough on a lightly
floured counter. Stamp out circles
using a 3-inch/7.5-cm cookie cutter.
Make crescent shapes by cutting away
a fourth of each circle. Re-roll the
trimmings to make about 25 crescents.

5 Place the crescents on the
prepared cookie sheets. Prick the
surface of each crescent with a fork.

6 Lightly whisk the egg white in a
small bowl and brush it over the
cookies. Dust with extra superfine
sugar, if you like.

7 Bake in a preheated oven,
400°F/200°C, for 12–15 minutes.
Transfer the cookies to a wire rack to
cool and crisp before serving.

coconut flapjacks

makes sixteen

1 cup butter, plus extra
    for greasing
1 cup raw brown sugar
2 tbsp light corn syrup
3½ cups rolled oats
1 cup dry unsweetened coconut
⅓ cup chopped candied cherries

COOK'S TIP

The flapjacks are best stored in
an airtight container and eaten
within 1 week. They can also be
frozen for up to 1 month.

VARIATION

For plain flapjacks, heat
3 tablespoons superfine sugar,
3 tablespoons light corn syrup,
and ½ cup butter in a pan over
low heat until the butter has
melted. Stir in 1¾ cups rolled
oats or oat flakes until combined,
then transfer to a greased cookie
sheet, and bake as above.

1 Lightly grease a 12 x 9-inch/
30 x 23-cm cookie sheet with
a little butter.

2 Heat the butter, raw brown sugar,
and light corn syrup in a large
pan over low heat until just melted.

3 Stir in the oats, shredded coconut,
and candied cherries and mix well
until evenly combined.

4 Place the mixture on the prepared
cookie sheet. Spread evenly
across the cookie sheet and level the
surface by pressing with a spatula.

5 Bake the flapjack in a preheated
oven, 325°F/170°C, for about
30 minutes, until golden.

6 Remove from the oven and
let cool on the cookie sheet for
10 minutes.

7 Cut the mixture into 16 pieces
using a sharp knife.

8 Carefully transfer the flapjack
squares to a wire rack and let
cool completely.

peanut butter cookies

makes twenty

½ cup butter, softened, plus extra
   for greasing
½ cup chunky peanut butter
generous 1 cup granulated sugar
1 egg, beaten lightly
generous 1 cup all-purpose flour
½ tsp baking powder
pinch of salt
½ cup chopped unsalted
   natural peanuts

COOK'S TIP

For a crunchy bite and
sparkling appearance, sprinkle
the cookies with raw brown
sugar before baking.

VARIATION

For a change, use light molasses
sugar instead of granulated and
add 1 teaspoon apple pie
spice with the flour and
baking powder.

---

1 Lightly grease 2 cookie sheets.
with a little butter.

2 Beat the softened butter and
peanut butter together in a large
mixing bowl.

3 Gradually add the granulated
sugar and beat well.

4 Add the beaten egg, a little at a
time, beating after each addition
until thoroughly blended.

5 Strain the flour, baking powder,
and salt into the creamed peanut
butter mixture.

6 Add the chopped peanuts
and bring the mixture together
with your fingers to form a soft, sticky
dough. Wrap the cookie dough in
plastic wrap and chill in the refrigerator
for 30 minutes.

7 Form the dough into 20 balls
and place them on the prepared
cookie sheets, spaced well apart to
allow room to expand during cooking,
and flatten slightly with your hand.

8 Bake in a preheated oven,
375°F/190°C, for 15 minutes,
until golden brown. Transfer the
cookies to a wire rack and let cool
before serving.

apricot & cranberry tart

serves eight

DOUGH

1¼ cups all-purpose flour, plus extra
    for dusting

2 tbsp superfine sugar

½ cup butter, diced

1 tbsp water

FILLING

scant 1 cup sweet butter

1 cup superfine sugar

1 egg

2 egg yolks

⅓ cup all-purpose flour, sifted

1⅔ cups ground almonds

4 tbsp heavy cream

14½ oz/410 g canned apricot
    halves, drained

generous 1 cup fresh cranberries

1 To make the dough, place the flour and sugar in a bowl and rub in the butter with your fingertips until the mixture resembles bread crumbs. Add the water and bring the mixture together with your fingers to form a soft dough. Wrap in plastic wrap and chill in the refrigerator for 30 minutes.

2 Roll out the dough on a lightly floured counter and use it to line a 9½-inch/24-cm loose-based tart pan. Prick the base of the tart shell with a fork and chill in the refrigerator for 30 minutes.

3 Line the tart shell with foil and baking beans and bake in a preheated oven, 375°F/190°C, for

15 minutes. Remove the foil and baking beans and cook the tart shell for 10 minutes more.

4 To make the filling, cream the butter and sugar together in a bowl until light and fluffy. Beat in the egg and egg yolks, then stir in the flour, almonds, and cream.

5 Place the apricot halves and cranberries on the base of the tart shell and spoon the filling mixture over the top.

6 Bake in the preheated oven for about 1 hour, or until the topping is just set. Let cool slightly, then serve warm or cold.

pine nut tart

serves eight

DOUGH

1¼ cups all-purpose flour, plus extra
   for dusting

2 tbsp superfine sugar

½ cup butter, diced

1 tbsp water

FILLING

1½ cups farmer's cheese

4 tbsp heavy cream

3 eggs

½ cup superfine sugar

grated rind of 1 orange

1 cup pine nuts

1 To make the dough, place the flour and sugar in a bowl and rub in the butter with your fingertips until the mixture resembles bread crumbs. Add the water and bring the mixture together with your fingers to form a soft dough. Wrap in plastic wrap and chill in the refrigerator for 30 minutes.

2 Roll out the dough on a lightly floured counter and use it to line a 9½-inch/24-cm loose-based tart pan. Prick the base of the tart shell with a fork and chill for 30 minutes.

3 Line the tart shell with foil and baking beans and bake in a preheated oven,t 375°F/190°C, for 15 minutes. Remove the foil and baking beans and cook the shell for 15 minutes more.

4 To make the filling, beat the farmer's cheese, cream, eggs, sugar, orange rind, and half of the pine nuts together in a bowl. Pour the filling into the tart shell and sprinkle with the remaining pine nuts.

5 Reduce the oven to 325°F/160°C and bake the tart for about 35 minutes, or until the filling is just set. Let cool before removing from the pan and serving.

VARIATION

Replace the pine nuts with sliced
almonds, if you like.

---

italian bread pudding

serves four

1 tbsp butter, for greasing

2 small eating apples, peeled, cored, and sliced into rings

generous ⅓ cup granulated sugar

2 tbsp white wine

3½ oz/100 g bread, sliced with crusts removed (slightly stale French baguette is ideal)

1¼ cups light cream

2 eggs, beaten

pared rind of 1 orange, cut into thin sticks

VARIATION

For a change, try adding some dried fruit, such as apricots, cherries, or dates, to the pudding, if you like.

1 Grease a 5-cup/1.2-litre deep ovenproof dish with the butter.

2 Arrange the apple rings across the base of the dish, overlapping them, then sprinkle half of the sugar over the apples.

3 Pour the wine over the apples. Add the bread slices, pushing them down with your hands to flatten them slightly.

4 Mix the cream with the eggs, the remaining sugar, and the orange rind and pour the mixture over the bread. Set aside to soak for 30 minutes.

5 Bake the pudding in a preheated oven, 350°F/180,°C for about 25 minutes, until golden and set. Remove from the oven and serve.

COOK'S TIP

Some varieties of eating apples are better for cooking than others. Among the most suitable are Blenheim Orange, Cox's Orange Pippin, Egremont Russet, Granny Smith, Idared, James Grieve, Jonagold, Jonathan McIntosh, Northern Spy, and Winesap.

crème brûlée tarts

serves six

DOUGH

1¼ cups all-purpose flour, plus extra
   for dusting

2 tbsp superfine sugar

½ cup butter, diced

1 tbsp water

FILLING

4 egg yolks

¼ cup superfine sugar

1¾ cups heavy cream

1 tsp vanilla extract

raw brown sugar, for sprinkling

1 To make the dough, place the flour and sugar in a bowl and rub in the butter with your fingertips until the mixture resembles bread crumbs. Add the water and bring the mixture together with your fingers to form a soft dough. Wrap in plastic wrap and chill in the refrigerator for 30 minutes.

2 Divide the dough into 6 pieces. Roll out the dough on a lightly floured counter and use it to line 6 tartlet pans, 4 inches/10 cm wide. Prick the base of the dough with a fork and chill in the refrigerator for 20 minutes.

3 Line the tart shells with foil and baking beans and bake in a preheated oven, 375°F/190°C, for 15 minutes. Remove the foil and beans and cook for 10 minutes more, until crisp and golden. Let cool.

4 Meanwhile, make the filling. Beat the egg yolks and sugar together in a bowl until pale. Heat the cream and vanilla extract in a pan until just below boiling point, then pour onto the egg mixture, whisking constantly.

5 Return the mixture to a clean pan and bring to just below a boil, stirring constantly until thick. Do not let the mixture boil or it will curdle.

6 Let the mixture cool slightly, then pour into the tart shells. Let cool, then chill in the refrigerator overnight.

7 Sprinkle the tarts with brown sugar. Place under a preheated hot broiler for a few minutes. Let cool, then chill for 2 hours before serving.

baked pears with cinnamon

serves four

4 ripe pears

2 tbsp lemon juice

¼ cup light brown sugar

1 tsp ground cinnamon

5 tbsp lowfat spread

finely grated lemon rind, to decorate

lowfat custard, to serve

1 Core and peel the pears, then slice them in half lengthwise, and brush all over with the lemon juice to prevent them from discoloring. Arrange the pear halves, cored sides down, in a small nonstick roasting pan.

2 Place the sugar, cinnamon, and lowfat spread in a small pan over low heat, stirring constantly, until the sugar has completely dissolved. Keep the heat as low as possible to prevent too much water evaporating from the lowfat spread as it starts to get hot. Spoon the sugar mixture over the pears.

3 Bake in a preheated oven, 400°F/200°C, for 20–25 minutes, or until the pears are tender and golden, occasionally spooning the sugar mixture over the fruit during the cooking time.

4 To serve, heat the lowfat custard until it is piping hot and spoon a little onto 4 warmed dessert plates, then arrange 2 pear halves on each plate.

5 Decorate the pears with a little finely grated lemon rind and serve immediately.

pavlova

serves six

3 egg whites

pinch of salt

¾ cup superfine sugar

1¼ cups heavy cream,
    lightly whipped

fresh fruit of your choice, such as
    raspberries, strawberries, peaches,
    passion fruit, or ground cherries

1 Line a cookie sheet with a sheet of baking parchment. Whisk the egg whites with the salt in a large bowl until they form soft peaks.

2 Whisk in the superfine sugar, a little at a time, whisking well after each addition until all of the sugar has been incorporated and the meringue is smooth and glossy.

3 Spoon three-fourths of the meringue onto the cookie sheet, forming an 8-inch/20-cm circle.

4 Place spoonfuls of the remaining meringue all around the edge of the circle to join up to make a neat nest shape.

5 Bake in a preheated oven, 275°F/140°C, for 1¼ hours.

6 Turn the heat off, but leave the pavlova in the oven until it is completely cold.

7 Place the pavlova on a serving dish. Spread with the lightly whipped cream, then arrange the fresh fruit on top. Do not add the cream and fruit too far in advance, or the pavlova will go soggy.

mincemeat & grape jalousie

serves four

1 tbsp butter, for greasing

1lb 2 oz/500 g ready-made puff
   pastry dough, thawed if frozen

14½ oz/410 g jar sweet mincemeat

1 cup grapes, seeded and cut
   in half

1 egg, beaten lightly

raw brown sugar, for sprinkling

COOK'S TIP

Puff pastry has a high proportion
of fat—this is what gives it its
characteristic layered appearance
and light, crisp texture. However,
this also makes it more fragile
than other types of pastry, so
handle it as lightly and as
little as possible.

VARIATION

For an enhanced festive flavor,
stir 2 tablespoons of sherry into
the mincemeat

1 Lightly grease a cookie sheet
with the butter.

2 Roll out the puff pie dough on a
lightly floured counter and cut
into 2 rectangles.

3 Place one dough rectangle on the
prepared cookie sheet and brush
the edges with water.

4 Combine the mincemeat and
grapes in a mixing bowl. Spread
the mixture evenly over the dough
rectangle on the cookie sheet, leaving
a 1-inch/2.5-cm border.

5 Fold the second pie dough
rectangle in half lengthwise,
and cut a series of parallel lines across
the folded edge with a sharp knife,
leaving a 1-inch/2.5-cm border.

6 Open out the second rectangle
and lay it over the mincemeat
filling. Press the edges of the pie
dough together to seal.

7 Flute and crimp the edges of the
dough with your fingers. Lightly
brush with the beaten egg to glaze
and sprinkle with raw brown sugar.

8 Bake in a preheated oven,
425°F/220°C, for 15 minutes.
Reduce the heat to 350°F/180°C and
cook for 30 minutes more, until the
jalousie is well risen and golden brown.

9 Transfer to a wire rack to cool
completely before serving.

treacle tart

serves eight

9 oz/250 g ready-made unsweetened
 pastry dough, thawed if frozen

1 cup light corn syrup

scant 2 cups fresh white
 bread crumbs

½ cup heavy cream

finely grated rind of ½ lemon
 or orange

2 tbsp lemon or orange juice

homemade custard, to serve

COOK'S TIP

Syrup is notoriously sticky and so
can be quite difficult to measure.
Dip the spoon in hot water first
and the syrup will slide off it
more easily and completely.

VARIATION

Use the dough trimmings to
create a lattice pattern on top of
the tart, if you wish.

---

1 Roll out the pie dough on a lightly floured counter and use it to line an 8-inch/20-cm loose-based tart pan, reserving the dough trimmings. Prick the bottom of the tart shell with a fork and chill in the refrigerator for 30 minutes.

2 Cut out small shapes from the reserved dough trimmings, such as leaves, stars, or hearts, to decorate the top of the tart.

3 Combine the light corn syrup, bread crumbs, heavy cream, grated lemon or orange rind, and lemon or orange juice in a bowl.

4 Pour the mixture into the tart shell and decorate the edges of the tart with the dough cut-outs.

5 Bake in a preheated oven, 375°F/190°C, for 35–40 minutes, or until the filling is just set.

6 Let the tart cool slightly in the pan Turn out and serve hot or cold with homemade custard.

cheese & ham loaf

makes one loaf

6 tbsp butter, diced, plus extra
  for greasing

generous 1½ cups self-rising flour

1 tsp salt

2 tsp baking powder

1 tsp paprika

1¼ cups grated sharp cheese

scant ½ cup chopped smoked ham

2 eggs, beaten lightly

⅔ cup milk

COOK'S TIP

This tasty bread is best eaten on
the day it is made, as it does not
keep for very long.

1 Grease a 1-lb/450-g loaf pan
  with a little butter and line the
base with baking parchment.

2 Strain the flour, salt, baking
  powder, and paprika into a large
mixing bowl.

3 Rub in the butter with your
  fingertips until the mixture
resembles fine bread crumbs. Stir
in the cheese and ham.

4 Add the beaten eggs and milk
  to the dry ingredients in the
bowl and mix well.

5 Spoon the cheese and ham
  mixture into the prepared pan.

6 Bake in a preheated oven,
  350°F/180°C, for about 1 hour,
or until the loaf is well risen.

7 Let the bread cool in the pan,
  then turn out, and transfer to
a wire rack to cool completely.

8 Cut the bread into thick slices
  to serve.

onion tart

serves four

9 oz/250 g ready-made pie dough,
   thawed if frozen

3 tbsp butter

generous ⅓ cup chopped bacon

1 lb 9 oz/700 g onions,
   thinly sliced

2 eggs, beaten

scant ⅔ cup freshly grated
   Parmesan cheese

1 tsp dried sage

salt and pepper

VARIATION

To make a vegetarian version
of this tart, replace the bacon
with the same amount of
chopped mushrooms.

---

1 Roll out the pie dough on a
lightly floured counter and use
it to line a 9½-inch/24-cm loose-based
tart pan.

2 Prick the base of the tart shell
with a fork and chill in the
refrigerator for 30 minutes.

3 Meanwhile, heat the butter in a
pan, add the bacon and onions,
and sweat over low heat for about
25 minutes, or until tender. If the onion
slices start to brown, add 1 tablespoon
of water to the pan.

4 Add the beaten eggs to the
onion mixture and stir in the
grated cheese and sage. Season with
salt and pepper to taste.

5 Spoon the onion mixture into the
prepared tart shell, spreading it
out evenly over the base.

6 Bake in a preheated oven, 350°F/
180°C, for 20–30 minutes, or
until the filling has just set and the
pastry is crisp and golden.

7 Let the tart cool slightly in the
pan. Serve warm or cold.

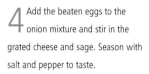

sun-dried tomato rolls

makes eight

⅓ cup butter, melted and cooled
   slightly, plus extra for greasing
generous 1½ cups strong white
   bread flour, plus extra
   for dusting
½ tsp salt
1 envelope active dry yeast
3 tbsp lukewarm milk
2 eggs, beaten lightly
1¾ oz/50 g sun-dried tomatoes in
   oil, drained and finely chopped
milk, for brushing

VARIATION

Add some finely chopped
anchovies or olives to the dough
in step 5 for extra flavor,
if you wish.

---

1 Lightly grease a cookie sheet
   with a little butter.

2 Strain the flour and salt into a
   large mixing bowl. Stir in the dry
yeast, then pour in the melted butter,
milk, and eggs. Bring together to form
a dough.

3 Turn the dough out onto a
   lightly floured counter and knead
for about 5 minutes, until smooth.
Alternatively, use an electric mixer with
a dough hook.

4 Place the dough in a greased
   bowl, cover, and let rise in a
warm place for 1–1½ hours, or until
the dough has doubled in size.

5 Punch down the dough for
   2–3 minutes. Knead the sun-dried
tomatoes into the dough, sprinkling
the counter with extra flour, because
the tomatoes are quite oily.

6 Divide the dough into 8 even-size
   balls and place them on the
prepared cookie sheet. Cover and let
rise for about 30 minutes, or until the
rolls have doubled in size.

7 Brush the rolls with milk and
   bake in a preheated oven,
450°F/230°C, for 10–15 minutes,
or until they are golden brown.

8 Transfer the tomato rolls to a
   wire rack and let cool slightly
before serving.

spicy bread

makes one loaf

2 tbsp butter, diced, plus extra
   for greasing

generous 1½ cups self-rising flour

¾ cup all-purpose flour, plus extra
   for dusting

1 tsp baking powder

¼ tsp salt

¼ tsp cayenne pepper

2 tsp curry powder

2 tsp poppy seeds

⅔ cup milk

1 egg, beaten lightly

COOK'S TIP

If the bread looks as though it is browning too much, cover it with foil for the remainder of the cooking time.

1 Lightly grease a cookie sheet with a little butter.

2 Strain the self-rising flour and the all-purpose flour into a mixing bowl with the baking powder, salt, cayenne, curry powder, and poppy seeds.

3 Rub in the butter with your fingertips until the mixture resembles bread crumbs.

4 Add the milk and beaten egg and bring together with your fingers to form a soft dough.

5 Turn the dough out onto a lightly floured counter, then knead lightly for a few minutes.

6 Shape the dough into a circle about 2 inches/5 cm deep and mark a cross shape on the top with a sharp knife.

7 Bake in a preheated oven, 375°F/190°C, for 45 minutes.

8 Remove the bread from the oven, transfer to a wire rack, and let cool. Serve the bread cut into chunks or slices.

mini focaccia

serves four

2 tbsp olive oil, plus extra
    for brushing
2½ cups strong white bread flour,
    plus extra for dusting
½ tsp salt
1 envelope active dry yeast
1 cup lukewarm water
1 cup pitted green or black olives,
    cut in half

TOPPING
2 red onions, sliced
2 tbsp olive oil
1 tsp sea salt
1 tbsp fresh thyme leaves

1 Lightly brush several cookie
sheets with olive oil. Strain the
flour and salt into a large bowl, then
stir in the yeast. Pour in the olive oil
and water and bring together with
your fingers to form a dough.

2 Turn the dough out onto a lightly
floured counter and knead for
about 5 minutes. Alternatively, use an
electric mixer with a dough hook and
knead for 7–8 minutes.

3 Place the dough in a greased
bowl, cover, and let stand in a
warm place for about 1–1½ hours, or
until it has doubled in size.

4 Punch down the dough for
1–2 minutes. Knead half of the
olives into the dough. Divide the
dough into fourths and then shape the
fourths into circles. Place them on the
cookie sheets and push your fingers
into them to achieve a dimpled effect.

5 To make the topping, sprinkle the
red onions and remaining olives
over the dough circles. Drizzle the olive
oil over the top of the onions and
olives, then sprinkle with the sea salt
and thyme leaves. Cover and let rise
for 30 minutes.

6 Bake in a preheated oven,
375°F/190°C, for 20–25 minutes,
or until the focaccia are golden.

7 Transfer to a wire rack and let
cool before serving.

VARIATION
Use this quantity of dough
to make 1 large focaccia,
if you like.

---

soda bread

makes one loaf

1 tbsp butter, for greasing

generous 2 cups all-purpose flour,
    plus extra for dusting

generous 2 cups whole-wheat flour

2 tsp baking powder

1 tsp baking soda

2 tbsp superfine sugar

1 tsp salt

1 egg, beaten lightly

generous 1¾ cups plain yogurt

VARIATION

For a fruity version of this soda
bread, add ¾ cup of raisins to the
dry ingredients in step 2.

---

1 Grease a cookie sheet with the butter and dust lightly with flour.

2 Strain both types of flour, the baking powder, baking soda, sugar, and salt into a large bowl, and add any bran remaining in the strainer.

3 In a pitcher, beat together the egg and yogurt and pour the mixture into the dry ingredients. Mix well, bringing together to form a soft and sticky dough.

4 Knead the dough for a few minutes on a lightly floured counter until smooth, then shape it into a large round about 2 inches/ 5 cm deep.

5 Transfer the dough to the prepared cookie sheet. Mark a cross shape on top with a sharp knife.

6 Bake in a preheated oven, 375°F/190°C, for 40 minutes, or until the bread is golden brown.

7 Transfer the loaf to a wire rack and let cool completely. Cut into slices to serve.

garlic bread rolls

makes eight

1 tbsp butter, for greasing

12 garlic cloves

1½ cups milk, plus extra
    for brushing

3½ cups strong white bread flour,
    plus extra for dusting

1 tsp salt

1 envelope active dry yeast

1 tbsp dried mixed herbs

2 tbsp sunflower oil

1 egg, beaten lightly

rock salt, for sprinkling

1 Lightly grease a cookie sheet with the butter.

2 Peel the garlic cloves and place them in a pan with the milk. Bring to a boil over low heat and simmer gently for 15 minutes. Let cool slightly, then place in a blender or food processor, and process into a paste.

3 Strain the flour and salt into a large mixing bowl and stir in the dry yeast and mixed herbs.

4 Add the garlic-flavored milk, sunflower oil, and beaten egg to the dry ingredients, mix well, and bring together with your fingers to form a dough.

5 Turn the dough out onto a lightly floured counter and knead lightly for a few minutes until smooth and soft.

6 Place the dough in a greased bowl, cover, and let rise in a warm place for about 1 hour, or until doubled in size.

7 Punch down the dough for 2 minutes. Divide into 8, shape into rolls, and place on the cookie sheet. Score the top of each roll with a knife, cover, and leave for 15 minutes.

8 Brush the rolls with milk and sprinkle rock salt over the top.

9 Bake in a preheated oven, 425°F/220°C, for 15–20 minutes. Transfer the rolls to a wire rack to cool before serving.

cheese & mustard biscuits

makes eight

4 tbsp butter, diced, plus extra
    for greasing
generous 1½ cups self-rising flour,
    plus extra for dusting
1 tsp baking powder
pinch of salt
1¼ cups grated sharp cheese
1 tsp mustard powder
⅔ cup milk, plus extra for brushing
pepper

1 Lightly grease a cookie sheet with a little butter.

2 Strain the flour, baking powder, and salt into a mixing bowl. Rub in the butter with your fingertips until the mixture resembles bread crumbs.

3 Stir in the grated cheese, mustard powder, and enough milk to form a soft dough.

4 Knead the dough very lightly on a lightly floured counter. Flatten it out with the palm of your hand to a depth of about 1 inch/2.5 cm.

5 Cut the dough into 8 wedges with a knife. Brush the wedges with a little milk and sprinkle with pepper to taste.

6 Bake in a preheated oven, 425°F/220°C, for 10–15 minutes, until the biscuits are golden brown.

7 Transfer the biscuits to a wire rack and let cool slightly before serving.

This is a Parragon Publishing Book
This edition published in 2004

Parragon Publishing
Queen Street House
4 Queen Street
Bath BA1 1HE, UK

ISBN: 1-40543-616-6

Printed in China

NOTE

Cup measurements in this book are for American cups. This book also uses
imperial and metric measurements. Follow the same units
of measurement throughout; do not mix imperial and metric.
All spoon measurements are level: teaspoons are assumed to be 5 ml and
tablespoons are assumed to be 15 ml. Unless otherwise stated, milk is assumed
to be whole milk, eggs and individual vegetables such as potatoes are medium,
and pepper is freshly ground black pepper.

The times given for each recipe are an approximate guide only because the
preparation times may differ according to the techniques used by different
people and the cooking times may vary as a result of the type of oven used.

Recipes using raw or very lightly cooked eggs should be
avoided by infants, the elderly, pregnant women, convalescents, and anyone
suffering from an illness.